Miles and Miles of Reptiles

I'm the Cat in the Hat
in my Crocodile Car.
We're off to find reptiles
wherever they are.

The Cat in the Hat's Learning Library™
introduces beginning readers to basic non-fiction. If your child can read these lines, then he or she can begin to understand the fascinating world in which we live.

Learn to read. Read to learn.

This book comes from the home of

THE CAT IN THE HAT

RANDOM HOUSE, INC.

For a list of books in **The Cat in the Hat's Learning Library,** *see the back endpaper.*

To John, Vivian, Charlie,
Johnny, and Melody, with love.
—T.R.

The editors would like to thank
BARBARA KIEFER, Ph.D.,
Charlotte S. Huck Professor of Children's Literature,
The Ohio State University, and
JIM BREHENY,
Director, Bronx Zoo,
for their assistance in the preparation of this book.

Visit us on the Web!
www.randomhouse.com/kids
www.seussville.com

Educators and librarians, for a variety of teaching tools, visit us at
www.randomhouse.com/teachers

Library of Congress Cataloging-in-Publication Data
Rabe, Tish.
Miles and miles of reptiles : all about reptiles / by Tish Rabe ; illustrated by
Aristides Ruiz and Joe Mathieu.
   p. cm. — (The Cat in the Hat's learning library)
Includes index.
ISBN 978-0-375-82884-3 (trade) — ISBN 978-0-375-92884-0 (lib. bdg.)
1. Reptiles—Juvenile literature. I. Ruiz, Aristides, ill. II. Mathieu, Joe, ill. III. Title.
QL644.2.R315 2009 597.9—dc22 2008006929

Printed in the United States of America
16 15 14 13 12 11 10 9 8 7

Miles and Miles of Reptiles

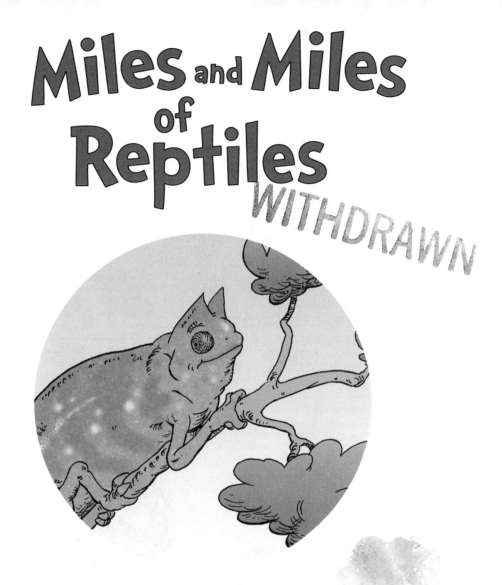

by Tish Rabe

illustrated by Aristides Ruiz and Joe Mathieu

The Cat in the Hat's Learning Library™

Random House 🏠 New York

I'm the Cat in the Hat
in my Crocodile Car.
We're off to find reptiles
wherever they are.

We'll find lizards and turtles,
then travel for miles
to see snakes, alligators,
and real crocodiles!

here are thousands of reptiles.

I show some to you.

ur mother will not

ind at all if I do.

Reptiles breathe air.
Most lay eggs on land.

Some slither.

8

Some swim.

Some run on hot sand.

Some reptiles have teeth.
Some reptiles have tails.
All reptiles have skin
that is covered in scales.

First, let's meet some lizards.
Count them and you'll find
more lizards than all
other reptiles combined!

Lizards have eyelids
that open and close.
Most lizards, you'll see,
on each foot have five toes.

10

When lizards are hungry,
some things that they eat
are plants, insects, snails,
and other types of meat.

There are all kinds of lizards.
Would you ever think
that there is a lizard
that's known as a skink?

This is a glass lizard.
It looks like a snake.
But call it a snake
and you make a mistake!

The world's biggest lizard
is here in our wagon.
It can grow ten feet long.
It's a Komodo dragon.

13

Reptiles are cold-blooded,
but I have been told
this does not mean reptiles
have blood that is cold.

It means that their
temperature changes a lot.
They get cold when it's cold.
They get hot when it's hot.

How do lizards get warm?
Why, thank you for asking.
They lie in the sun.
And that is called basking.

15

Meet my friend the chameleon.
He's hiding right here.
He changes his color
when danger is near.

When he's scared, he turns dark
and he stays out of sight,
but his colors turn bright
when he's ready to fight!

A chameleon's tail
has a powerful grip.
It holds on to things
so that it won't slip.

One eye can look one way
while one looks the other.
One eye looks at me.
One looks at my brother!

kuh-MEEL-yun
= chameleon

On the Galápagos Islands
we'll see something new:
iguanas! They're lizards.
Here's what they do.

They swim in the waves
and when they are done,
they crawl on the rocks
and get warm in the sun.

These lizards are geckos.
Aren't they pretty?
They live in the desert,
rain forest, and city.

They have pads on their feet
that are perfect for gripping.
They can climb up a wall—
even glass—without slipping!

Why are they named "gecko"?
Thing One and I know!
Some chirp and squeak
and it sounds like "geck-OH!"

Come meet some snakes!
When they move on the groun[d]
the scales on their skin
help them slither around.

A snake's jaw is loosely attached on each side. This means it can open its mouth very wide.

A snake smells with its tongue.
He is showing us how.
See it flick in and out?
He is smelling right now!

How do snakes avoid danger
so they can survive?
Here are some things
that help snakes stay alive.

Snakes may have stripes,
spots, or rings on their skin.
They can hide in plain sight.
Their skin helps them blend in.

Some, like a vine snake,
can fool you and me.
It looks like a vine
hanging down from a tree.

If you hear a rattlesnake's
tail start to rattle,
it means "I might bite you!"
so you'd better skedaddle!

A cobra's a snake
that's not very polite,
and that is because of
its poisonous bite.

When it's angry, a cobra
spreads out its big hood.
If you see it, you'll know
things are not looking good.

Fangs hang from its jaw
and punch holes in the skin.
Then a poison called venom
begins to flow in.

Now meet the turtles!
Each one has a shell.
This hard shell protects it
and does so quite well.

Turtles heat up
in a nice, sunny spot,
then slide into the water
when they get too hot.

Turtles are toothless,
so they cannot chew.
They swallow food whole.
That's all they can do.

Here is a tortoise!
I happen to know
this reptile eats grass
and it moves very slow.

It looks like a turtle,
but I understand
a turtle lives in the wat
a tortoise on land.

"TOR-tus" = TORTOISE

bout the tortoise
discovered one thing—
ach year of its life,
s shell grows a new ring.

Turtles have four legs,
but sea turtles like these
have flippers to swim
through the water with ease.

They lay eggs on land
and each mom somehow knows
which beach SHE was hatched on,
so that's where she goes!

When the babies are hatched,
the shells on their backs
are so soft, they are helpless
if something attacks!

We measured these babies.
They're so very small,
their shells are just three inches long
and that's all!

1 2 3 4 5 6 7

On the Florida coast
in a swamp or lagoon,
you may see a crocodile
swimming by soon.

Crocodiles have sharp teeth
and they walk on four legs.
Their feet have sharp claws.
Their young hatch from eggs.

There are crocs that can eat
till they're filled up, and then
it could be months—even years—
before they eat again!

Alligators and crocodiles
look alike, as you see.
That's because they belo[ng]
to the same family.

We looked at them closel[y]
and here's what we saw—
the gator's teeth hang
over its lower jaw.

GATOR

CROC

They both live near water,
and these reptiles glide

by swinging their powerful
tails side to side.

CROC

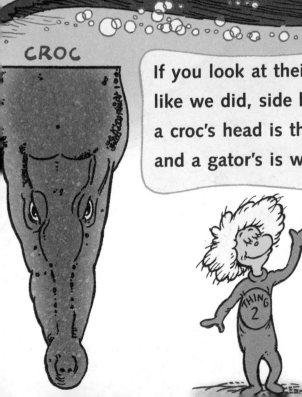

If you look at their heads
like we did, side by side,
a croc's head is thin
and a gator's is wide.

GATOR

They mate in the wate[r]
Then, we understand,
the female comes out
to lay eggs up on land.

She digs a deep nest.
Then she lays her eggs in i[t]
laying sixty or so,
about one every minute.

INSIDE

When the babies are hatched, this is how small they are— each one weighs as much as Thing One's candy bar.

1.76oz **50g**

CANDY BAR

1.73oz **49g**

Reptiles are everywhere•
Just look, you might se•
one down on the groun•
or up high in a tree.

They come in all shapes
and all colors and sizes,
and you will discover
they're full of . . .

surprises!

GLOSSARY

Avoid: To stay away from.

Fangs: Special teeth that are hollow for the purpose of injecting venom.

Flippers: Broad, flat limbs that are used for swimming.

Glands: Organs that remove substances from blood.

Lagoon: A shallow lake or pond connected to a large body of water.

Poisonous: Containing a substance that can harm or kill.

Scales: Thin, flat plates that protect the skin of all reptiles.

Slither: To slide or glide.

Temperature: The degree to which something is hot or cold.

Venom: The poison in some snakes (and other animals) that is passed on to prey through a bite or sting.

FOR FURTHER READING

olorful Chameleons! by Michelle Knudsen, ustrated by Bryn Barnard (Random House, *Step to Reading,* Step 3). All about chameleons, from hat they eat to why they change color. For grades -3.

fe-Size Reptiles by Hannah Wilson (Sterling, *Life- ze Series*). Photographs and descriptions of reptiles. or grades 1–3.

ne Tiny Turtle by Nicola Davies, illustrated by Jane napman (Candlewick, *Read and Wonder*). A simple ory about the life of a loggerhead turtle. For ndergarten to grade 2.

eptile by Colin McCarthy (Dorling Kindersley, *yewitness Books*). Great photographs of reptiles and escriptions of their lives. For grades 2 and up.

nakes, Salamanders and Lizards by Diane L. Burns, ustrated by Linda Garrow (NorthWord Books for oung Readers, *Take-Along Guide*). A field guide with :tivities and safety tips. For grades 2 and up.

S-Snakes! by Lucille Recht Penner, illustrated by ater Barrett (Random House, *Step into Reading,* Step . A basic introduction to snakes. For grades 1–3.

INDEX

The Cat in the Hat's Learning Library™

Clam-I-Am!

Fine Feathered Friends

A Great Day for Pup

Hurray for Today!

I Can Name 50 Trees Today!

If I Ran the Rain Forest

Inside Your Outside!

Is a Camel a Mammal?

Miles and Miles of Reptiles

My, Oh My—a Butterfly!

Oh Say Can You Say DI-NO-SAUR?

Oh Say Can You Say
What's the Weather Today?

Oh Say Can You Seed?

Oh, the Pets You Can Get!

Oh, the Things You Can Do
That Are Good for You!

On Beyond Bugs!

One Cent, Two Cents,
Old Cent, New Cent

There's a Map on My Lap!

There's No Place Like Space!

A Whale of a Tale!

Wish for a Fish

Would You Rather Be a Pollywog?

Coming in Fall 2010:

Ice Is Nice!